The Brief History of

The Holocaust

The Rise of Antisemitism in Nazi Germany,
Auschwitz, and Hitler's Genocide on Jewish
People Fueled by Fascism

(1941-1945)

Disclaimer

1

Introduction

The **Holocaust**, also called **Shoah**, **Shoa** or **Shoah** (Hebrew: השואה *Ha-Shoah*), was the systematic persecution and genocide of Jews by the Nazis and their allies before and during World War II. During the domination by Nazi Germany, between 5.1 and 6 million European Jews were murdered. Most of the killing took place in death camps in gas chambers and in mass executions by Einsatzgruppen.

Table of contents

3

The term Holocaust

Etymology

The word *holocaust* means "burnt sacrifice" and is derived from the Ancient Greek word ὁλόκαυστον (*holokauston*), which literally means "completely burned.

In ancient times this was a term for a burnt offering to a deity. The word *holocaust* also existed in this sense in Middle Dutch in the 14th century, but subsequently fell into disuse.

Meaning shift and application

According to the *Oxford English Dictionary,* the earliest known English mention of the word *holocaust* in the sense of mass murder dates from 1833, when Scottish journalist Leitch Ritchie, in a description of the wars of the French medieval king Louis VII, recounted that the latter "once made a holocaust of thirteen hundred people in a church," a mass murder by fire of the inhabitants of Vitry-le-François in 1142. In the early 20th century, prior to the Second World War, Winston Churchill and other contemporary writers used it to refer to the Armenian

Genocide during the First World War. There is a reference to the Armenian Genocide in the title of the poem "The Holocaust" (published as a booklet in 1922) and the book *The Smyrna Holocaust* (1923) is about the burning and mass murders of Armenians.

The first time the word "holocaust" was applied in English to the Nazi genocide was in 1942, but it was not until the 1950s that historians introduced the historical term "the Holocaust" (with a definite article and capital letter).

It is generally assumed that the American television series *Holocaust* (by Jewish-American director Gerald Green), first broadcast in the USA from 16 to 19 April 1978 and later also in numerous European countries, made the most significant contribution to popularising the term in this sense in most languages, including Dutch. Van Dales *Groot Woordenboek der Nederlandse Taal*, tenth edition (1976), mentions only the meaning of *burnt offering* under Holocaust.

Other terms

Jews in particular use the term *Shoah* (שואה = *disaster, total destruction*) as an alternative to Holocaust. Thus the annual commemoration is called Yom Hashanah.

The leaders of the NSDAP themselves used the term *Endlösung der Judenfrage* (final solution of *the Jewish question*), a term that had existed since the 19th century, but only in the course of 1941 was it given the meaning of 'extermination of the European Jews', and with the Wannsee Conference (20 January 1942) was it given a more definitive form.

Discussion about counting non-Jewish victims

In addition to about 6 million Jews, the Nazis also murdered about 5 million other people. Scholars are divided on the question of whether the term "Holocaust" should be applied to all victims of National Socialist mass murder, with some using it as a synonym for Shoah or the Endlösung der Judenfrage, while others (wish to) also include the murder of Roma and Sinti (gypsies), Poles and other Slavs, the death of Soviet prisoners of war, homosexual men, Jehovah's Witnesses, the handicapped, the mentally handicapped, and political opponents. There

7

is also the question whether the entire period from 1933 to 1945 should be considered or only the war period after 1939 and especially 1941.

- **Contra:** Czech-Israeli historian Yehuda Bauer argues that the Holocaust should only be about Jews, because the Nazis would have intended to completely exterminate only the Jews and not the other groups.

  Counting non-Jewish victims of the Nazis in the Holocaust is rejected by several individuals such as Jewish Holocaust survivor Elie Wiesel and organizations such as Yad Vashem, an Israeli state institution in Jerusalem established in 1953 to commemorate Holocaust victims.

  According to them, the word originally referred to the extermination of the Jews, and the Jewish Holocaust was a crime of such magnitude, totality and specificity, and the climax of a long history of European anti-Semitism, that it should not be placed in a general category with the other crimes of the Nazis.

- **Pro:** British historian Michael Burleigh and German historian Wolfgang Wippermann argue that although all Jews were victims, the Holocaust transcended the boundaries of the Jewish community - other people shared in the tragic fate of victimization.

Former Hungarian Minister for Roma Affairs László Teleki applies the term *Holocaust* to both the murder of Jews and Roma by the Nazis and their allies. In *The Columbia Guide to the Holocaust,* American historians Donald Niewyk and Francis Nicosia use the term for Jews, Gypsies, and the disabled.

American historian Dennis Reinhartz has claimed that Gypsies were the main genocide victims in Croatia and Serbia during World War II and therefore calls it "the Balkan Holocaust 1941-1945".

Number of victims

Definition width, surveys and estimates

The exact number of victims is not known; various estimates are made on the basis of the available evidence. The total number depends mainly on which definition of "the Holocaust" is used.

According to Donald Niewyk and Francis Nicosia, the term is commonly defined as the mass murder of more than five million European Jews.

However, they also say that "not everyone finds this an entirely satisfactory definition".

According to British historian Martin Gilbert, the total number of victims was just under six million - about 78 percent of the 7.3 million Jews in occupied Europe at the time.

Timothy D. Snyder wrote that "the term Holocaust is sometimes used in two different ways: for all German murder programs during the war or for any form of oppression of the Jews by the Nazi regime." Wichert ten Have and Maria van Haperen of the NIOD Institute for War, Holocaust and Genocide Studies argued that the goal of the Holocaust was "the murder of European Jews and the destruction of the Jewish people as such," but added that "other authors argue that other persecuted groups

11

such as the Roma should also be considered victims of the Holocaust."

Broader definitions also include the two to three million Soviet prisoners of war who died as a result of mistreatment by Nazi racist policies, two million non-Jewish ethnic Poles killed by the conditions of Nazi occupation, 90,000 to 220,000 Roma, 270.000 mentally and physically handicapped in the German eugenics program, 80,000 to 200,000 Freemasons, 20,000 to 25,000 Slovenes, 5,000 to 15,000 homosexuals, 2,500 to 5,000 Jehovah's Witnesses, and 7,000 Spanish Republicans, bringing the death toll to about 11 million.

The broadest definition would also include six million Soviet citizens who died as a result of war-related hunger and disease, bringing the death toll to 17 million. A research project conducted from 2000 to 2013 by the United States Holocaust Memorial Museum estimated that 15 to 20 million people across Europe died or were confined in camps or other conditions.

There are also differences of opinion about the periodization. Microsoft Encarta states that the Holocaust occurred from the Machtergreifung on 30 January 1933 until V-day on 8 May 1945 (surrender of Germany), divided into two periods: January 1933 to September 1939 (social exclusion of the Jews) and from September 1939 to May 1945 (total extermination of the Jews).

Others say that the Holocaust did not begin until the fall of 1941, when the Nazis actually proceeded to carry out mass murder of the Jews.

Jewish victims

The most reliable estimates put the total number of Jews murdered at between 5.1 million and just over 6 million.

Non-Jewish victims of the Nazi regime

Besides Jews, other groups were also systematically murdered, including homosexuals, Esperantists, Gypsies, "economically unworthy", Russians, ethnic Poles, the handicapped, Jehovah's Witnesses, Free Bible Researchers, trade unionists, Freemasons, Communists, Spanish Republicans, Serbs, Quakers and people who opposed the Nazis. The total number of murdered non-Jews is estimated at 5 to 11 million people.

13

Background

Property

Why exactly the Nazis and their allies proceeded to murder Jews, homosexuals, Gypsies and 'economically unworthy' people such as the physically and mentally handicapped on a large scale, and how the civilian population largely went along with this, is the subject of debate.

This was argued by Daniel Goldhagen, among others, with his book *Hitler's willing executioners*. What is clear is that Adolf Hitler's fierce anti-Semitism was the 'engine' that made National Socialism guilty of ethnic cleansing or genocide.

A genocide on such a large scale was only possible because a number of factors were at play simultaneously in parts of Europe, especially Germany:

- The presence or stable installation of a dictatorship without control or existing separation of the various state powers.

- Geographically widespread latent and sometimes virulent anti-Semitism, strongly anchored in the Christian culture of Europe.

The run-up to the Holocaust

At the end of World War I, the economy of the German Empire was exhausted and the army was on the verge of collapse. Eventually, soldiers and workers unleashed the November Revolution, deposing the Kaiser and proclaiming the Weimar Republic. The Social Democratic interim government first concluded an armistice and eventually the Treaty of Versailles with the Allies.

Millions of Germans felt deeply humiliated that they had lost the battle. To pass on the responsibility for the defeat, the German military leadership invented the Dolkstoot legend, according to which the German army had not lost the war at all, but had been betrayed by the Marxists.

Since Karl Marx was a Jew, Hitler believed that Marxism was a Jewish conspiracy and that the humiliation of Germany was therefore the fault of the Jews. In *Mein Kampf* (1924), he claimed that the war would not have been lost if the Germans had put "twelve to fifteen thousand of these Hebrew folk beggars through a few poison gas attacks."

Anti-Semitism and anti-Ziganism had always been part of the NSDAP party program, in which Hitler's ideas played an increasingly important role. This anti-Semitism was further fuelled by the post-war hyperinflation of 1919-23 because of the idea that Jews were often in the banking and business world.

Not only Hitler, but many leaders of his party were also anti-Semites. Julius Streicher's radical party newspaper, *Der Stürmer, was* at the top of the list. The Nazis saw the Jews as 'bacilli' that 'sickened' and 'undermined' the German nation.

18

When Adolf Hitler came to power in 1933, there was certainly latent anti-Semitism in the country, which was exploited by the NSDAP and the SA. Yet this was certainly not the same anti-Semitism as that of the NSDAP. Anti-Semitism in Germany was more economic in nature and certainly did not go so far as to want to exterminate or remove the Jews. Many Jews integrated into German society and were no longer seen as Jews.

The anti-Semitism of the NSDAP was mainly influenced by anti-Semitism in Austria and Sudetenland, which was much more radical. Hitler himself had lived for years in Vienna, where German speakers felt threatened by the growing presence of non-German speakers and Jews.

Here emerged groups which argued that there was a "Jewish race" which was inferior to the "Germanic race" and which "undermined" this race and its purity. This was the anti-Semitism propagated by the NSDAP, which already advocated more radical solutions in the 19th century.

The Nuremberg Race Laws

The road to the Holocaust/Shoa began with government and party encouraged harassment by radical elements. This harassment included name-calling, ridicule, molestation, and occasionally murder. When things got too outrageous, there was "intervention" from above, after which the government "appeased" the radicals with anti-Semitic measures to "prevent further violence." This eventually culminated in the "Nuremberg Laws" of 1935.

This included a package of discriminatory measures and regulations determining who was and who was not a German or a Jew. These new laws deprived Jews of their civil rights and prohibited marriage between Jews and non-Jews. In the 1930s, the Nazi party was very popular and anti-Semitism was "taken at face value," even by those who were not anti-Semites.

It was also assumed that the ideology would weaken over time as the NSDAP ruled, which actually seemed to happen during the 1936 Olympics. However, the NSDAP had deliberately stopped the harassment in order to keep up appearances during the Games. After 1936, the measures and harassment continued.

On 10 November 1938, following the murder of Vom Rath, Reichskristallnacht, or Kristallnacht for short, took place. Thousands of plain-clothes SA men raided Jewish homes and shops, set fires in synagogues and beat up Jews.

This led to the exclusion of the Jews from the economy and the imposition of a 1 billion mark fine on the Jewish community, since according to the government the Jews were the instigators. Foreign criticism was countered with the statement that this was an expression of the healthy popular opinion, the "Gesundes Volksempfinden".

The "solution"

During the 1930s and early 1940s the Nazis consulted widely and employed various strategies to find and achieve a 'solution to the Jewish question'.

These can be roughly divided into assimilation, emigration, deportation and extermination. Like the other three, extermination was considered, but for a long time considered undesirable or impracticable. Only when the other plans had failed did this become the *final solution* (*Endlösung*) in 1941.

Migration

In the years 1938-1941 a solution was worked out in which Jews would be sent to a certain area. One option was British Palestine, another was Madagascar. Especially after the victory over France, many Nazis would adhere to the Madagascar plan, but this was not feasible while the war lasted. The British Navy controlled the sea and the Germans did not dare put too much pressure on the French to make them give up their colony.

The eventual occupation of the island by Allied troops caused this plan to disappear from the agenda once and for all. A further step toward genocide was the idea of using Jews as hostages to keep the United States out of the war.

The attack on the Soviet Union opened up new possibilities for the Nazi philosophers. Now they could send all the Jews from Greater Germany and its satellites to Siberia, where they would "perish."

After all, if they had it "too easy," the Jews might be a threat in a new Jewish state.

Therefore, according to the Nazis, they were better off dying. The first camps for Jews arose in the east, but after the defeat of Moscow it became clear that the option of deporting the Jews to Soviet territory was not feasible for the time being.

The Ha'avara-Abkommen (Ha'avara is Hebrew for transfer; Abkommen is German for agreement) is an agreement made on 25 August 1933 after three months of negotiations between the Jewish Agency, the Zionist Vereinigung für Deutschland and the German Ministry of
23

Economic Affairs. This agreement laid down how Jewish Germans who wanted to emigrate to Palestine could take part of their assets with them.

Ghettos

Meanwhile, in occupied Poland, the district leaders of eastern districts such as Wartheland and Gdansk-West Prussia began to make their districts "Judenrein" (free of Jews) by deporting Jews to the General-Gouvernment (the German-initiated Polish rump state). The new lands were seen as an opportunity to create an ideal Nazi society.

This of course included the "removal" of "undesirable elements", including Jews. A certain competition developed between the district leaders as to who had the most Nazi-ified district.

This created ghettos in the Polish cities: overcrowded, fenced-off residential areas where the Jews had to live under the most unhygienic conditions.

Murder

Extermination or extermination was increasingly seen as the best option; besides, deporting and imprisoning the Jews cost money and food. Various methods were considered. Shooting them "cost too many bullets", and moreover was "mentally stressful" for the executioners. The use of explosives was also considered, but this led to scattered body parts, which could also lead to nervous disorders among the camp staff. Gassing was considered the solution.

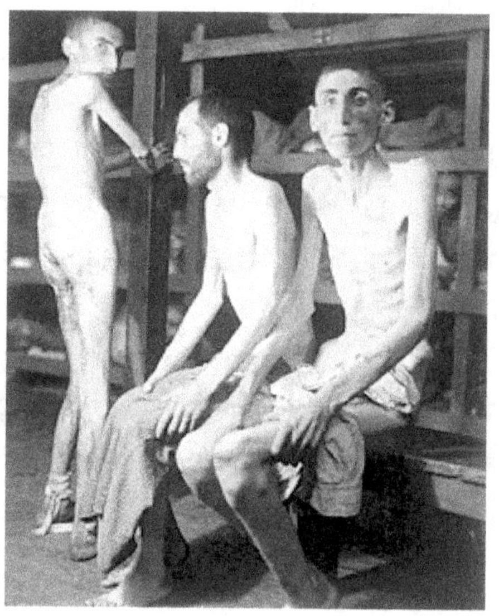

Initially, this was done with carbon monoxide. Special *gas vans* were used. The Jews were told that they were being "transported" by lorry, and the exhaust fumes were then fed into the lorry. The lorry then drove on to a mass cemetery.

In late August or early September 1941, the first test with the insecticide Zyklon B was conducted in Auschwitz.

The next day the effectiveness was checked, and it turned out that a large proportion of the prisoners were still alive. The dose was then increased. The SS ordered prisoners to dispose of the bodies and burn them in the crematorium.

26

After this first experiment, a second gassing with Zyklon B was carried out on a transport with Russian prisoners of war. Zyklon B had already been used for deaeration, but the extreme toxicity of the substance gave acting commandant of Auschwitz Karl Fritzsch the idea to use it for gassing prisoners.

Final Solution

Hitler took the decision to destroy European Jewry (the so-called *Endlösung der Judenfrage*, or *Final Solution to the Jewish Problem*) in all likelihood in September 1941. At the Wannsee Conference in a villa on Lake Wannsee near Berlin in January 1942, the logistical implementation of the decision was discussed. Adolf Eichmann, one of the most notorious actors in the Holocaust, was among those present.

From that moment on one could speak of a planned and systematic genocide, in so far as it was not already underway.

Incidentally, a systematic genocide was already taking place earlier: the actions of the infamous *Einsatzgruppen*, who immediately behind the advancing Wehrmacht on the Eastern Front rounded up all Jews and communists and murdered them in mass executions. This was organised by order from Berlin and began as early as July 1941, when Hitler invaded the Soviet Union.

Extermination, concentration and transit camps

Extermination camps

Extermination camps were set up for the *Final Solution*. These camps were intended for deliberate and systematic murder. An extermination camp is a camp where most of the prisoners were gassed immediately upon arrival. This fate befell the sick, the elderly and children. The prisoners who were kept alive were given various tasks in order to keep the camp running.

These activities varied from heavy labour to service in the kitchens, for example. Eventually these prisoners would also be gassed.

These camps were located in the eastern part of the Reich (in present-day Poland) and were consequently also liberated by the Red Army.A total of seven camps were designated as extermination camps, six of them in Poland and one in Belarus. These seven camps were:

- Chełmno
- Bełżec

* Treblinka II
* Sobibór
* Maly Trostenets
* Majdanek, also concentration camp
* Auschwitz II (Auschwitz-Birkenau)

Concentration camps

In addition to extermination camps, the Nazis had a large number of concentration camps, such as Dachau (near Munich) and Buchenwald (near Weimar). A concentration camp is not the same as an extermination camp.

As the name implies, a concentration camp is a work camp where prisoners were concentrated. Most people died there because of the heavy work, malnutrition, diseases and mistreatment. These labor camps can be compared with the so-called "gulags" in Soviet Siberia. In the 1940s many concentration camps were also equipped with gas chambers, where prisoners were gassed.

Transit camps

In addition to the concentration and extermination camps there were also so-called transit camps. These were camps set up to gather people and then transport them in special trains to the extermination camps on a weekly schedule. Westerbork is an example of a transit camp in the Netherlands.

In Belgium, the existing Kazerne Dossin in Mechelen was used for this purpose. In the French camp of Drancy, north of Paris, approximately 65 thousand Jews were held during the Second World War before being transported to the Auschwitz extermination camp. Theresienstadt was also a transit camp.

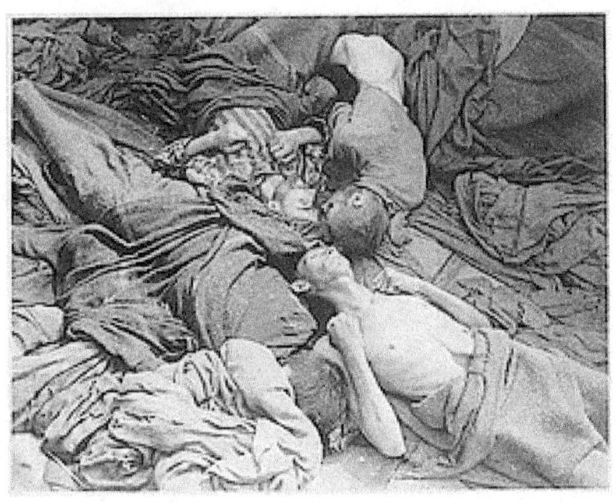

Death marches

During the advance of the Soviet troops the last remaining camps, mainly in Poland and the Czech Republic, were closed down from the end of 1944. The Nazis often decided not to leave the prisoners behind, but to force them to march west.

Those who were too weak, too old or too young were simply executed. These so-called death marches once again claimed countless victims. It is estimated that more than 250,000 people were killed.

Attitude towards the persecution of Jews

In Nazi Germany and the European territories occupied by the Axis Powers, the response to the persecution of Jews and other groups varied depending on a number of factors. In some regions, especially where civilian administrations were formed and ideologically driven SS ruled, persecution was carried out with greater force than areas with military regimes, where it was given less priority and resistance made more sense.

Jews also had a better chance of survival in countries where many non-Jews also tried to go into hiding, for example to avoid conscription into the *Einsatzgruppen*, so that it was easier to make use of an existing network. Where the Nazis met with active or passive resistance, the persecution of the Jews could sometimes be partially sabotaged. Where the population was more actively involved, however, a larger percentage of Jews were exterminated.

Jewish resistance

The Jews themselves revolted a number of times. In 1943, the Warsaw Ghetto revolted. In Auschwitz in October

1944, Jewish prisoners blew up a crematorium with smuggled in explosives. In October 1943, there was a successful uprising in Sobibór: eleven German SS officers, including the sub-commander, were killed, and about three hundred of the six hundred prisoners escaped. About sixty of them survived the war. The escape prompted the Nazis to close the camp, probably for fear of revelation. In the Netherlands quite a few politically left-oriented (socialist and communist) Jews were in the resistance. They also often refused to wear the hated Jewish star.

On 19 April 1943, the same day the Warsaw Ghetto revolted, the twentieth train convoy in Belgium was attacked by three Young Resistance members. This transport of Jews had departed from Mechelen with destination Auschwitz. Armed with one revolver, a hurricane lamp and red paper, three students (Georges Livschitz, Robert Maistriau and Jean Franklemon) from the Atheneum in Uccle forced the train to stop on the Mechelen-Leuven railway line between Boortmeerbeek and Haacht. This is a unique fact in the history of the Holocaust. Nowhere else in Europe was a liberation operation carried out on a transport of Jews during the Second World War.

When attempts were made to persecute the small Jewish community in Denmark, they were protected and eventually transported to Sweden. Finland, allied with Germany for opportunistic reasons, refused to persecute or extradite Jews. Japan protected the few Jews who were in Japanese or occupied territory. When the Germans wanted Bulgarian Jews to wear stars, the entire population proudly wore them. Later attempts by the Germans and Bulgarian anti-Semites were also blocked.

Some well-known people who actively opposed the Holocaust:

- Hans Calmeyer
- Giorgio Perlasca
- Witold Pilecki
- Oskar Schindler
- Chiune Sugihara
- Raoul Wallenberg

There was and is much speculation about the motives of those who actively or passively resisted. Genuine sympathy for the Jewish fellow men and indignation about their treatment will in most cases have played a role to a greater or lesser extent. Others tried to keep their own house clean and did not want to be tried as war criminals after the war. Others took advantage of the situation and enriched themselves on the refugees.

Netherlands

More than one hundred thousand of the Dutch Jews, approximately 75% of the Jews living in the Netherlands at the start of the occupation, did not survive the war. This percentage was much higher than in Belgium (40%) and France (25%), for example.

It is often assumed in public debate that this is primarily due to Dutch citizens' indifference to the fate of their Jewish compatriots, but a historical study by Pim Griffioen and Ron Zeller, *Persecution of Jews in the Netherlands, France and Belgium, 1940-1945* (Amsterdam: Boom, 2011) has shown this to be a misunderstanding.

In fact there was a complex combination of factors that caused this percentage to be so high in the Netherlands. One important factor was that during the war years the Netherlands had a *Zivilverwaltung* (civil administration) and not a *Militärverwaltung (military administration)* as in Belgium and France. The civil administration was therefore formed by ideologically driven SS who wanted to continue the total extermination of the Jews. Although public protest in the Netherlands was greater, with the February Strike as a prime example, this was also much harder repressed by the occupier.

The Dutch civil servants also made the population registers available to the occupying forces. The exact civil registration officials even listed them as 'emigrated'. Prior to the analysis of the population registers by the Nazis, the then Dutch Ministry of the Interior conducted extensive research into the historical origins of Dutch family names.

Family names of Dutch Jews were included and explained in a separate section. A summary of this research was published in book form by the investigating government official during the occupation. The book itself gives no clear indication of the reason for the investigation.

Five thousand Roma in the Netherlands died as a result of the gypsy persecution.

Belgium

About twenty-five thousand Belgian Jews were victims,
about 40% of all Jews in the country. Most of the Jews had
only recently moved to Belgium/ fled from Eastern Europe
because of increasing anti-Semitism there; they were more
distrustful of the government than in the Netherlands.

Unlike the Netherlands, there was not as much public
protest against the persecution of Jews, but there was an
extensive network of people in hiding much earlier,
because in 1941 Belgium had to provide troops for the
Arbeitseinsatz (forced labour in Germany), from which non-
Jews also tried to escape.

This relatively small number was also partly due to the fact
that Belgium had a *Militärverwaltung (military
administration)* during the German occupation. The
protests against the persecution of the Jews, although not
as strong, were therefore more effective than in the
Netherlands. It was not until 1944 that the administration
was transformed into a *Zivilverwaltung* (civil
administration). The transit camp, the Dossin Barracks
where the Jews were assembled before being transported

to the extermination camps in Poland, was located in Mechelen, halfway between Antwerp and Brussels, where most of the Jews lived.

Luxembourg

Luxembourg was initially under military occupation, but this was replaced in August 1940 by a civil administration under Gustav Simon, a situation similar to the Netherlands. The reason was ideological; Luxembourg was seen by the Nazis as an ethnic German territory that should be incorporated into Germany.

Of the 3800 Jews living in Luxembourg in 1940, 2000 fled immediately after the invasion, leaving 1800 Jews on 10 May 1940. They were subjected to occupational bans and various other anti-Jewish measures.

During the first year of occupation, 619 Jews were expelled by the Gestapo and deported to Spain, but because that country did not accept them either, they were dragged from place to place. What happened to them is not clear, but there is a big chance that some of them died because of the bad circumstances.

From October 1941, Simon's anti-Semitic policies began to become more violent with the destruction of synagogues and deportations. A further 683 Jews were deported, of whom only 43 eventually returned. On 17 June 1943 Simon declared that Luxembourg was 'judenrein'.

An estimated 1200 Jewish Luxemburgers did not survive the war.

France

In France, approximately 25% of all Jews were deported. Anti-Semitism was stronger in France than in the Netherlands; there was less public protest against the persecutions and the Vichy regime, which retained civil authority throughout France, took all manner of anti-Jewish measures on its own initiative. As in Belgium, however, the Germans had a military administration in occupied France that gave no priority to the persecution of the Jews, while the southeast remained unoccupied. The Vichy regime also resisted when the Nazis wanted to deport native French Jews in March 1943.

The military occupying forces gave in and as a result no Holocaust trains ran from France to the east for months. Immigrant Jews, on the other hand, were handed over to the Germans. After the occupation of the previously unoccupied part of France in November 1942 (Operation Anton), large numbers of Jews fled to the Italian-occupied zone, which also became unsafe when the Germans took it over in September 1943. Thereafter, both French and immigrant Jews in France were exposed to persecution until German authority over France collapsed in the summer of 1944.

Romania

In Romania, the radically anti-Semitic Iron Guard formed a
government together with the army in 1940. This
government was characterised by violence against Jews,
sometimes with fatal results. The disturbances were so
serious that army chief Marshal Ion Antonescu expelled
the Guard from the government in 1941. Romania allied
itself with Germany, but the situation seemed to improve
for the Romanian Jews, and anti-Semitic measures were
only very sporadically introduced in Wallachia. This
moderation was apparent, however.

Antonescu did want to remove the Jews from Romanian
society, but was opposed to the violent looting by the Iron
Guard that was destroying the country. To this end he
collaborated with Adolf Eichmann and others. Although
Antonescu sometimes stopped the German transports, he
also allowed hundreds of thousands of other Jews to be
sent to the concentration camps.

In impoverished Moldavia in particular, the population
enthusiastically participated in the persecution of the Jews.

Hungary

The Holocaust in Hungary took place in four phases: mild discrimination (1920-1938), severe discrimination (1938-1941), violence and forced labour (1941-1944), active extermination (1944-1945). Hungary had shrunk considerably after the First World War, so that most of the 'ethnic' non-Hungarian population groups ended up outside the borders. This made the Jews within the new borders the largest minority, with 5% of the population in 1920.

They constituted a very successful economic minority: 60% of all doctors, 51% of all lawyers, 39% of all engineers and chemists outside government service, 34% of all publishers and journalists, and 29% of all artists identified with Judaism in terms of religion. This caused envy among the rest of the population, and the Reich Regent Horthy openly declared himself to be anti-Semite and blamed them for Hungary's post-World War I territorial wars.

Another factor was that prominent figures in the Hungarian Raden Republic, such as Bela Kun, were of (partly) Jewish origin.

49

Anti-Semitic measures had already been introduced in the 1920s, including a numerus clausus for Jews in university courses: henceforth only 5% of all students were allowed to be Jewish, in accordance with their population percentage.

In the 1930s Horthy faced pressure from an increasingly strong anti-Semitic opposition from the Arrow Cross and smaller Nazi parties. To take the wind out of the sails of these groups, Horthy began to pursue a more repressive anti-Jewish policy. Anti-Jewish legislation based on the Nuremberg Race Laws followed in 1938. The first anti-Jewish law (1938) established maximum percentages for Jews in certain occupational groups. The second anti-Jewish law (1939) determined that people with 2 or more Jewish grandparents were considered Jewish, tightened the maximum percentages, excluded them from journalism and government altogether, and denied them their (already severely restricted) voting rights. The third anti-Jewish law of 1941 prohibited marriages and sexual contact between Jews and non-Jews.

When Hungary took an active part in the war in 1941, there was open violence in the occupied territories. In addition to other ethnic minorities, Jews were the main victims. Hungarian Jews were forced to work on the construction and repair of infrastructure in both Hungary and the Soviet Union. Approximately 42,000 Jews did not survive this, due to both the poor conditions and deliberate murder by their Hungarian guards.

When Horthy tried to surrender to the Allies in 1944, the country was occupied by the Germans, who forced him to participate in the deportation of the Hungarian Jews.

These began in March 1944, and between 15 May and 30 June 1944 alone, 400,000 Jews were deported to the death camps. Horthy was eventually forced to appoint Ferenc Szálasi, the leader of the fascist Arrow Cross movement, as prime minister, after which he was forced to resign and imprisoned. Szálasi, while Soviet troops invaded the east of the country and besieged Budapest, in collaboration with Adolf Eichmann, sent some 80,000 more Jews to the death camps during these final months of war, where almost all of them died. In addition, 15,000 Jews together with communists and other opponents were murdered on the spot by the Arrow Crusaders.

51

Eventually, according to various estimates, between 80,000 and 255,000 of the 861,000 Jews in Hungary and the occupied territories would survive the war. This gave Hungary one of the lowest survival rates in Europe.

Baltic countries

In the Baltic states, the population took revenge for the support of many Jews to the Russian, and therefore communist, occupiers.

In both Romania and the Baltic States, moreover, people were aware of the large numbers of Jewish members of the Communist parties.

Soviet Union

Although anti-Semitism was prevalent in the Soviet Union, Jews were not legally discriminated against as it was not in line with the Bolshevik ideal of equality. There were estimated to be about 4 million Jews living in the western areas of the Soviet Union that would eventually be occupied by Germany and service allies, the former Pole region.

Approximately 3 million Jews were able to flee eastwards in time. The remaining 1 million were exposed to orchestrated massacres by the so-called Einsatzgruppen. Part of the population was in favour of the German occupiers and supported these actions or took an active part in them. On the other hand, there were also many who helped Jews.

Some of the Jews fell prey to massacres such as that at Babi Yar, while others were sent to the extermination camps. Many Jews joined the partisans and sabotaged both German war and occupation activities and measures against their fellow Jews. Estimates for the number of Jews killed in the Soviet Union remain unclear and vary widely; it is assumed that at least 700,000 Soviet Jews lost their lives.

Denmark

The resistance against the deportation of the Jews was strongest in Denmark. After it became known in September 1943 that the deportation of the Jewish population in Denmark was being prepared, a large-scale spontaneous rescue operation was launched in which all sections of the population participated. Great alarm was raised through synagogues, doctors, pastors and students who in turn informed the Jews.

The Jews were collected and transported to the Danish coast with everything that had wheels. The Jews were then taken by fishermen in boats across the Sound to neutral Sweden, with whom the Danes had already agreed that they would take care of the Danish Jews. Before the war, the Danish Jewish community numbered 8,200 people, of whom more than 95% survived the Nazis. After the war, the Danish Jews returned to their homeland and found their homes and property exactly as they had left them.

Croatia

In Croatia, the Jews were violently persecuted by the radical anti-Semitic Ustaša regime. However, many were able to escape during the first two months of occupation because the Croats first concentrated on the extermination and assimilation of the Serbs, more than half a million of whom disappeared.

Many Jews fled to the Italian-occupied territories because the Italian authorities did not implement Mussolini's anti-Semitic measures, or did so half-heartedly. Those Jews who stayed, however, fell prey to Croatian violence, after which they were sent to the camps with German efficiency. When Italy capitulated in 1943, Croatia occupied these areas and those Jews who could not flee in time were deported.

Italy

In Italy, most of the army commanders and police officers refused to persecute the Jews. Most of the victims fell after the Italian surrender on 8 September 1943. Of the nearly sixty thousand Italian Jews before the war, nearly eight thousand lost their lives, most of them in the Auschwitz concentration camp.

Albania

Albania is the only country where more Jews lived after the Second World War than before. The country formed a personal union with Italy, which discriminated against Jews but was otherwise half-hearted in its persecution. The Albanian government refused to hand over the names of the Jewish population to the German occupier, and Jewish refugees from Austria and the Balkan countries were hospitably received.

Bulgaria

Bulgaria was allied with Germany for opportunistic reasons, and there was certainly an anti-Semitic breeding ground. Initially, the Bulgarians were not unwilling to accommodate the Germans. The anti-Semitic policy began with raids in the occupied territories, during which a few thousand people were sent to concentration camps. In 'old Bulgaria', the anti-Semites and Germans tried to make the Jews wear Jewish stars, as in the rest of Europe.

This failed because the entire population started wearing this pride. An attempt to deport several hundred Bulgarian Jews to the extermination camps stranded near the Bulgarian port of Samovit: the Bulgarian population demonstrated en masse and the transport was cancelled. Finally, from 1943, the king personally blocked attempts to deport the Jews, partly because he realised that the Axis would lose the war.

Japan

Several thousand Jews lived in Japan and territories occupied by Japan. China already had a small Jewish community, to which was added Russian-Jewish traders and refugees based in Manchuria. Although Japan was an ally of Germany, it followed its own agenda in Asia, in which anti-Semitism had no place. Indeed, many Japanese officials saw opportunities to develop the occupied territories with the help of Jews and Jewish capital. Some Chinese and Japanese diplomats in Europe, such as Chiune Sugihara, were able to issue transit visas for Jewish refugees until late 1940. Between 1938 and late 1941, about 20,000 Jewish refugees from Europe arrived in occupied Shanghai.

From 1942, Germany increased its pressure on Japan to hand over the Jews present in Shanghai or to take an active part in the Holocaust. Japan did not wish to comply, but it did develop a more repressive policy against the Jews. In February 1943, for example, it was decided to house all Jews who had arrived in the city after 1937 in what was to become the Shanghai Ghetto. Also, especially after the German invasion of the Soviet Union, more space was given to anti-Semitic and anti-Soviet campaigns by Russian anti-communists and fascists in both Manchuria and Shanghai. Many Jews from Manchuria felt threatened by this harassment and also ended up in Shanghai, and thus in the ghetto. Conditions for the Jewish refugees in the ghetto were bad. In the winter of 1943 there was not enough food. The ghetto was liberated by Chiang Kai-shek's troops on 3 September 1945. After the establishment of the State of Israel in 1948 almost all residents left the ghetto. Eventually about 2000 people died in the ghetto.

End and aftermath

In the course of 1944 and 1945 all camps were liberated by Allied troops. The prisoners were fed and given medical care, but the vast majority could not immediately be returned to their former homes due to all kinds of legal, logistical and infrastructural difficulties. Thousands of survivors remained in displaced persons camps until 1947, when they were accepted by a country or were able to obtain a new home and nationality of their own accord.

Emigration

Many Jews no longer wished to return to the societies from which they had been uprooted or expelled and sought refuge in the Aliyah Bet: they left Europe for the British Mandate area of Palestine in the hope of founding a nation state for themselves there.

However, this soon led to conflicts with the Arab-Muslim population of Palestine. UN Resolution 181 provided for a two-state solution, and during the 1948 war the newly founded Jewish state of Israel was able to conquer more than its share of territory. Although this created a land for Jews, it also created the Arab-Israeli conflict.

Judgement

The Allies decided to try the main leaders of the Nazi regime jointly in the Nuremberg Trials and several other trials (September 1945 to December 1949), with *the* Nuremberg Trial (20 November 1945 - 1 October 1946) indicting 24 leaders of the NSDAP. For this the Nuremberg Principles were drawn up, which were necessary to state that international law took precedence over national law, because much of what the Nazis had done was legal according to the German law of the time.

Even if something were legal or not punishable under national law, people still acknowledged the existence of fundemental 'higher' principles that had to be adhered to. It was also established that the argument that 'I was only carrying out orders' ('Befehl ist Befehl') did not absolve someone of responsibility for a crime, not even when this order came from (then) competent and recognized authority.

Jewish property

Of those who returned from the camps, many found their homes occupied and their property dispossessed.

Only a few succeeded in recovering their property, and then only after often years of litigation. The German government made payments to the State of Israel through the *Wiedergutmachung programme*.

Impact on international law

The Holocaust also had important consequences under international law. At the new global political consultative body, the United Nations, a consensus was reached that such a crime against humanity should never again go unpunished.

On 9 December 1948 the Genocide Convention was adopted by the UN: all signatory countries committed themselves to intervene militarily to end or prevent a genocide.

The Fourth Geneva Convention of 1949 laid out in more detail the rights of civilians and military personnel in conflict and the duty of warring parties to adhere to certain standards, which the international community would enforce.

Post-war discussions

After the war there was much scientific and social discussion about many aspects of the Holocaust, about questions such as why and how exactly it happened and what conclusions should be drawn.

Contemporary knowledge of the Holocaust

One of the major controversies is about which part of the German population in particular was aware of the concentration camps and what happened there during the war.

When, after the war, the extent of the Holocaust gradually came to light, some Germans are said to have been unaware of it (*Wir haben es nicht gewußt*, "We didn't know"), even though they themselves had directly or indirectly contributed to it.

Question of guilt

Closely related to the question of who knew what about the Holocaust is the question of who exactly should be blamed (and thus punished) for it. According to the

Kollektivschuldthesis (introduced by Swiss psychoanalyst Carl Gustav Jung), the entire German people were to blame, regardless of whether they knew anything about the systematic persecution of Jews and others, let alone collaborated in it. Others believe that only those who knew about and consciously collaborated were to blame. There is also the question of the extent to which 'Befehl ist befehl' can absolve someone of responsibility. In various postwar trials, the Allies eventually decided to try only the absolute top of the Nazi regime.

During the criminal trial in Jerusalem of Adolf Eichmann, one of the most important organizers of the Holocaust, the

American Jewish writer Hannah Arendt was struck by the fact that Eichmann did not come across as some sort of horrible monster, but as an insignificant individual who nevertheless appeared to have been able to devise the methods by which many millions of Jews could be murdered.

Arendt's thesis about the "banality of evil" is that evil is something banal, something that people often do with a shrug of their shoulders without thinking about how immoral they actually are.

Claims handling

After the war, the West German authorities developed compensation schemes to compensate Holocaust victims and their survivors for the damage they had suffered. Exactly who was eligible, and in what way, was the subject of debate. In the German Democratic Republic, there was no regulation at all until 1966.

The Jewish-American political scientist Norman Finkelstein, himself a child of Holocaust survivors, wrote the book *The Holocaust Industry* in 2000, in which he denounced practices designed to abuse these compensation schemes.

According to him, there are many individuals who falsely claim to be victims or survivors, or exaggerate their suffering for financial gain. Moreover, European guilt for the Holocaust is said to be unfairly exploited to silence any criticism of Israel or the American Jewish community. Holocaust museums also try to monopolize the suffering of Jews and exclude other victim groups.

Jewish assets

71

It was not until the 1990s that the issue of Jewish war assets was put on the agenda in the Netherlands and abroad. Research was carried out into property looted from Jews during the Second World War, dormant bank accounts and insurance policies. In the Netherlands it was concluded that the total sum involved was € 346.7 million, but that the individual claimants or their surviving relatives could no longer be traced.

These so-called "maror funds", named after the bitter maror, were distributed around the year 2000 to all Dutch Jews via a distribution key and were partly used for Jewish social purposes.

Predatory art

Art and other valuable objects that Jews living in the Netherlands had to surrender to the Liro bank on the orders of the Nazis ended up at various museums after the war and, in a few cases, even at the royal house. By 2015, only a handful of these works had been returned to their legal heirs. Sometimes the municipality had bought work from an NSB member. Only 70 years after the war did the realisation dawn that municipalities and museums should have actively investigated the provenance of works acquired around that time.

Another ongoing issue in the twenty-first century is the approximately 1,200 paintings owned by Jewish art dealer Jacques Goudstikker, which he was forced to sell to Hermann Göring. Only in 2006 did the Dutch government decide, on "moral grounds", to return 202 works to the heiress of Goudstikker, who died while fleeing the Netherlands in 1940.

In 2015, however, Goudstikker's last heiress is still taking legal action to recover the works, which have ended up in all kinds of museums in the Netherlands and abroad.

Holocaust denial

Certain groups deny that the Holocaust took place. These Holocaust deniers are also called negationists.

Some negationists claim that the number of Jewish victims traditionally cited is incorrect. They say that far fewer than six million Jews were killed and that most of the casualties were from starvation and from outbreaks of diseases such as typhoid and cholera.

73

It is also claimed that gas chambers (both mobile and stationary) were only used for disinfection purposes.

Denying, trivialising or justifying the Holocaust is prohibited and punishable in countries including Germany, Belgium, France, Australia, Canada, Switzerland, Poland, Hungary and Israel.

In contrast, a conference on Holocaust denial was held in Iran on December 11-12, 2006.

The then president Mahmoud Ahmadinejad had made several comments about the Holocaust that were condemned in other countries. Jewish intellectuals also participated in the conference.

Historikerstreit

In 1986 there was a fierce debate among German historians about how to place the Holocaust in a larger historical context. Ernst Nolte was of the opinion that the Gulag Archipelago and the mass murders committed by the Soviet Union were as bad as the Holocaust and that the German people did not really need to feel particularly guilty about what had happened.

74

Jürgen Habermas did not agree at all and reproached Nolte for trying to trivialize the horror of the Holocaust.

Archives

The Germans themselves kept archives of the victims of the Holocaust. The German archives are extremely detailed because the Nazis kept accurate records of all information. Much archive and other evidence was destroyed by Operation Sonderaktion 1005.

Among other things, the Dutch overview *In Memoriam* with the names of 100 thousand murdered Jews is based on this. In addition, the names of Jewish victims are included in the Jewish Monument.

The German town of Bad Arolsen, Hesse, is home to the enormous archive (about 47 million items, about 6 houses full of paper). This archive contains information about 17.5 million people and fills more than 27 kilometers of shelves. It consists of lists, inventories, personal descriptions, reports of medical experiments, ordinances, etc.

In particular, the entire bureaucracy of terror that the orderly Nazis maintained for their machinery of forced labor, deportation, and extermination. The complete archives from the Buchenwald and Dachau concentration camps can be found there. The appalling scale of the war and the official German killing machine becomes clear.

The "International Tracing Service", a department of the Red Cross, manages the archives. This service was set up after the war to trace missing persons. It was mainly used by survivors who needed evidence to obtain benefits. The archive was also kept closed for privacy reasons, also for researchers because the documents contain sensitive information about individuals, such as a person's political beliefs, about Jewish collaborators and how they were encouraged to participate, who had lice, what medical experiments were carried out, the nature of a mental handicap, who was accused of homosexuality, incest or paedophilia.

There was also the German fear of legal proceedings if that information were to be released. The possibility of legal action has since been barred.

Fundamental news that will adjust the history of the Holocaust is not expected when historians consult the archives. Researchers do hope to find more details to reconstruct the history of the horror.

On 24 April 2007, the Belgian Parliament ratified the Protocol giving scientists and researchers access to the archives on the deportations during the Second World War in Bad Arolsen (Germany). The opening of the archives was decided following negotiations between the member states of the International Commission of the International Investigation Service. Belgium, the Netherlands, Luxembourg, Germany, France, Great Britain, Italy, Israel, the United States of America, Greece and Poland are members of this International Commission.

The archive was opened to researchers and the general public at the end of November 2007.

On 7 October 2013, the Fritz Bauer Institut in Frankfurt made digitally available the witness statements in the first Auschwitz trial held in Frankfurt (1963-1965).